Who Look at Me

Painter unknown, *Portrait of a Gentleman*.
Bowdoin College Museum of Art, Brunswick, Maine.

JUNE JORDAN

Who Look at Me

ILLUSTRATED WITH TWENTY-SEVEN PAINTINGS

THOMAS Y. CROWELL COMPANY

NEW YORK

Gratitude is owing to Milton Meltzer;
in response to a book idea conceived by him,
and thanks to his encouragement and respect,
I undertook the creation of *Who Look at Me*.
The pictures for the book were chosen from a
collection assembled by him.

June Jordan

Photos: page 26, Barney Burstein; page 69,
Yale Joel, *Life* magazine, © Time, Inc.

Designed by Klaus Gemming

Manufactured in the United States of America

L.C. Card 69–13641

1 2 3 4 5 6 7 8 9 10

FOR CHRISTOPHER MY SON

Who would paint a people
black or white?

For my own I have held
where nothing showed me how
where finally I left alone
to trace another destination

A white stare splits the air
by blindness on the subway
in department stores
The Elevator

          (that unswerving ride
where man ignores the brother
by his side)

A white stare splits obliterates
the nerve-wrung wrist from work
the breaking ankle or
the turning glory
of a spine

Is that how we look to you
a partial nothing clearly real?

Charles Alston, *Manchild*.
Collection, Charles Gorham.

who see a solid clarity
of feature
size and shape of some
one head
an unmistaken nose

the fact of afternoon
as darkening
his candle eyes

Older men with swollen neck

(when they finally sit down
 who will stand up
 for them?)

I cannot remember nor imagine pretty
people treat me
like a doublejointed stick

WHO LOOK AT ME
WHO SEE

the tempering sweetness
of a little girl who wears
her first pair of earrings
and a red dress

the grace of a boy removing
a white mask he makes beautiful

Iron grill across the glass
and frames of motion closed or
charred or closed

lleen Browning, *Door Street*. Collection, Milwaukee Art Center,
lwaukee, Wis., gift of Mrs. Harry Lynde Bradley.

Eastman Johnson, *Southern Courtship*. Collection,
Mr. and Mrs. J. William Middendorf II, New York.

The axe lies on the ground
She listening to his coming sound

him
just touching his feet
powerful and wary

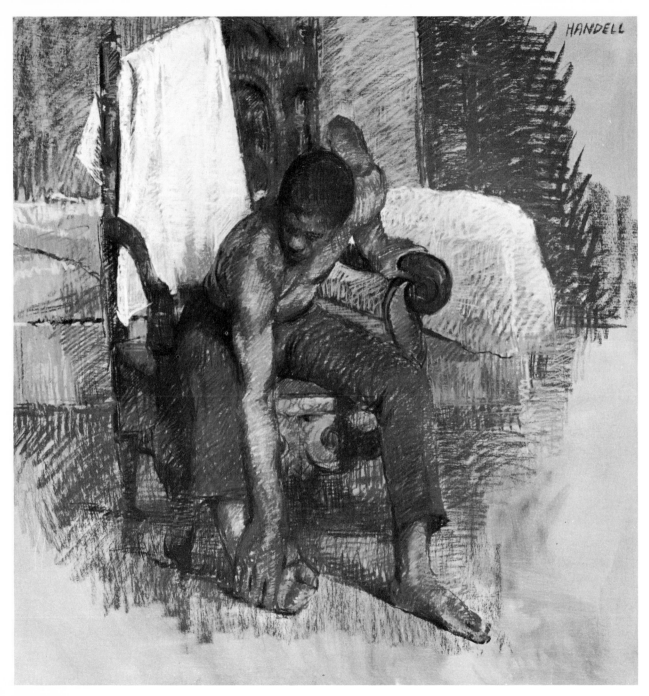

Albert Handell, *Tony Seated*. Syracuse University.

anonymous and normal
parents and their offspring
posed in formal

Charles Alston, *Family*. Collection, Whitney Museum
of American Art, New York.

Painter unknown, *Enigmatic Foursome*. Courtesy, New York
State Historical Association, Cooperstown, N.Y.

I am

impossible to explain
remote from old and new interpretations
and yet
not exactly

look at the stranger as

he lies more gray than black
on that colorquilt
that
(everyone will say)
seems bright beside him

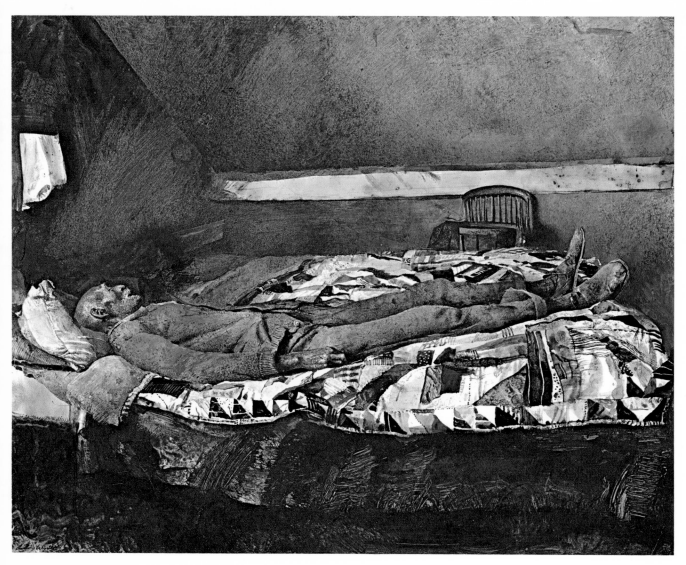

Andrew Wyeth, *Garret Room*. Courtesy, Mrs. Andrew Wyeth.

look
black sailors on the light
green sea the sky keeps blue
the wind blows high
and hard at night
for anyhow anywhere new

Winslow Homer, two sailors, detail from *Sloop, Bermuda.*
Metropolitan Museum of Art, Amelia B. Lazarus Fund, 1910.

Who see starvation at the table
lines of men no work to do
my mother ironing a shirt?

Who see a frozen skin the midnight
of the winter and the hallway cold
to kill you like the dirt?

where kids buy soda pop
in shoeshine parlors
barber shops so they can hear
some laughing

Who look at me?

Who see the children
on their street the torn down door the wall
complete an early losing
                                    games of ball
the search to find
a fatherhood a mothering of mind
a multimillion multicolored mirror
of an honest humankind?

look close
and see me black man mouth
for breathing (North and South)
A MAN

John Wilson, *Self-portrait.*
Courtesy, the artist.

Alice Neel, *Taxi Driver*. Courtesy, the artist.

Symeon Shimin, *Boy*.
Courtesy, the artist.
Collection, Frances P. Strauss.

Thomas Eakins, *Henry O. Tanner*.
The Hyde Collection, Glens Falls, N.Y.

I am black alive and looking back at you.

see me brown girl throat
that throbs from servitude

see me hearing fragile
leap
and lead a black boy
reckless to succeed
to wrap my pride
around tomorrow and to go
there
without fearing

Hughie Lee-Smith, *Boy with Tire*. Courtesy, Detroit Institute of Arts.

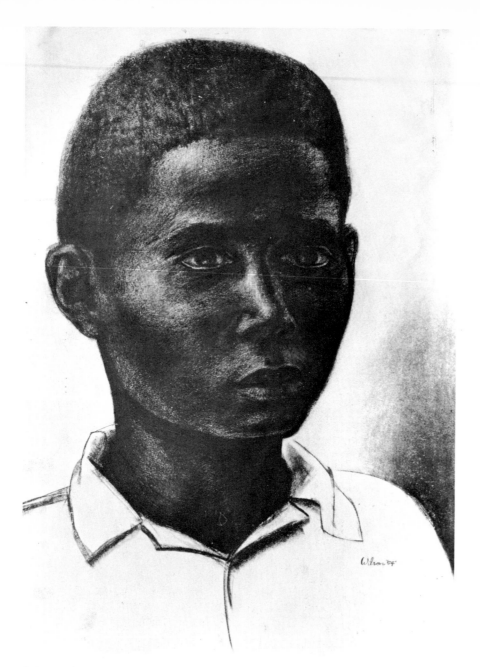

John Wilson, *Black Boy*. Courtesy, the artist.

see me darkly covered ribs
around my heart across my skull
thin skin protects the part
that dulls from longing

Who see the block we face
the thousand miles of solid alabaster space
inscribed keep off keep out don't touch
and Wait Some More for Half as Much?

To begin is no more agony
than opening your hand

sometimes you have to dance
like spelling
the word joyless

Thomas Eakins, *Negro Boy Dancing*. Metropolitan Museum of Art, Fletcher Fund, 1925.

Describe me broken mast
adrift but strong
regardless what may
come along

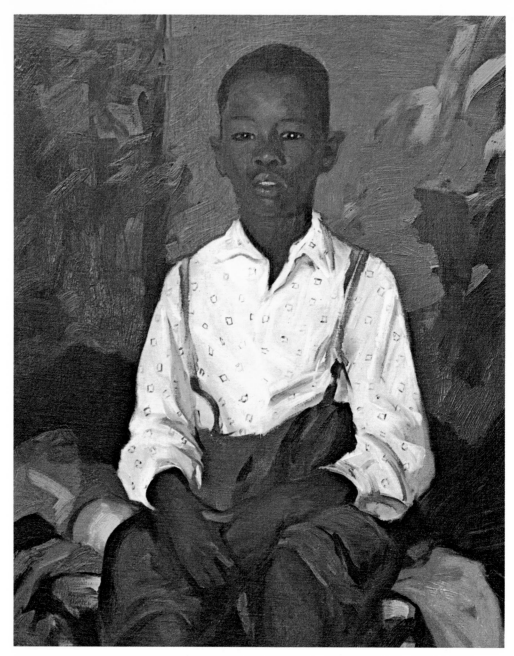

Robert Henri, *Sylvester*. Courtesy, Samuel Schwartz.

What do you suppose he hears
every evening?

I am stranded in a hungerland
of great prosperity

shelter happens seldomly and
like an accident
it stops

No doubt
the jail is white where I am born
but black will bail me out

We have lived as careful
as a church and prayer
in public

Ben Shahn, *Willis Avenue Bridge*. Collection, The Museum
of Modern Art, New York, gift of Lincoln Kirstein.

we reveal

a complicated past
of tinderbox and ruin
where we carried water
for the crops

we come from otherwhere

victim to a rabid cruel cargo crime

to separate and rip apart
the trusting members of one heart

my family

I looked for you
I looked for you

(slavery:) the insolence

Detail from *The Slave Market*

Painter unknown, *The Slave Market.* Museum of Art,
Carnegie Institute, Pittsburgh, gift of Mrs. John Barclay, Jr.

came to frontiers
of paralyze highways
freedom strictly underground

came here to hatred hope labor love
and lynchlength rope

came a family to a family

I found my father
silently despite the grieving
fury of his life

Afternoons he wore his hat
and held a walking stick

Andrew Wyeth, *Alexander Chandler*.
Collection, Mr. and Mrs. Robert Montgomery.

I found my mother
her geography
becomes our home

Edmund Archer, *The Organdy Collar*. Collection, Whitney Museum of American Art.

so little safety
almost nowhere like the place
that childhood plans
in a pounding happy space
between deliberate brown and clapping
hands
that preached a reaping to the wildly
    sleeping earth
brown hands that worked for rain a fire inside
    and food to eat
from birth brown hands
    to hold

Winslow Homer, *Sunday Morning in Virginia*. Cincinnati Art Museum.

New energies of darkness we
disturbed a continent
like seeds

and life grows slowly
so we grew

We became a burly womb
an evening harvest kept by prayers
a hallelujah little room

We grew despite the crazy killing scorn
that broke the brightness to be born

In part we grew
by looking back at you

that white terrain
impossible for black America to thrive
that hostile soil to mazelike toil
backbreaking people into pain

we grew by work by waiting
to be seen
black face black body and black mind
beyond obliterating
homicide of daily insult daily death
the pistol slur the throbbing redneck war
with breath

In part we grew
with heroes who could halt a slaveship
lead the crew
like Cinqué (son
of a Mendi African Chief) he
led in 1839
the Amistad Revolt
from slavehood forced
a victory he
killed the captain killed the cook
took charge
a mutiny for manhood
people
called him killer but

some
the Abolitionists
looked back at robbery
of person
murdering of spirit
slavery requires
and one
John Quincy Adams (seventy-three)
defended Cinqué who
by highest court decree
in 1841 stood free
and freely he returned
to Africa
victorious

Nathaniel Jocelyn, *Portrait of Cinqué*. Collection, New Haven Colony Historical Society.

In part we grew
grandmother husband son
together when the laborblinding day was done

In part we grew
as we were meant to grow
ourselves
with kings and queens no white man knew

Colleen Browning, *Mary-Mae* [The First Communion]. Courtesy, The Kennedy Gallery.

we grew by sitting on a stolen chair
by windows and a dream
by setting up a separate sail
to carry life
to start the song

to stop the scream

These times begin the ending of all lies
the fantasies of seasons start and stop
the circle leads to no surprise
for death does not bewilder
only life can kill can mystify can start
and stop like flowers ripening a funeral
like (people) holding hands across the knife
that cuts the casket to an extraordinary size

Tell the whiplash helmets GO!
and take away
that cream and orange Chevrolet
stripped to inside steel and parked
forever on one wheel

Set the wild dogs chewing up
that pitiful capitulation
plastic flower plastic draperies
to dust the dirt

Break the clothesline
Topple down the clotheslinepole

O My Lives Among The Wounded Buildings
should be dressed in trees and grass

we will no longer wait for want for watch
for what we will

Charles Alston, *Walking*. Courtesy, the artist.

We make a music marries room to room.

Eastman Johnson, *The Banjo Player*. Hirschl & Adler Galleries, New York City.

listen to that new girl
tears her party dress to sweep
the sidewalk as the elderly slow
preacher nears the mailbox in a black suit
emptyhanded

Although the world
forgets me
I will say yes
AND NO

Romare Bearden, *Mysteries.* Courtesy, Cordier–Ekstrom Gallery, New York City.

NO
to a carnival run by freaks
who take a life
and tie it terrible
behind my back

No One Exists As Number Two
If you deny it you should try
being someone number two

I want to hear something other than a single
ringing on the concrete

I grieve the sorrow roar the sorrow sob
of many more left hand or right
black children and white
men the mountaintop the mob
I grieve the sorrow roar the sorrow sob
the fractured staring at the night

Sometimes America the shamescape
knock-rock territory losing shape
the Southern earth like blood
rolls valleys cold gigantic
weeping willow flood
that lunatic that lovely land
that graveyard growing
trees remark where men
another black man
died he died again
he died

I trust you will remember how we tried to love
above the pocket deadly need to please
and how so many of us died there
on our knees.

Who see the roof and corners of my pride
to be (as you are) free?

WHO LOOK AT ME?

NOTES ABOUT THE ARTISTS

Charles Alston (1907–) was born in Charlotte, North Carolina, went to New York public schools, and earned his A.B. and M.A. at Columbia University. In the 1930's he directed the Harlem Art Workshop. Since 1950 he has taught at the Art Students League. His work has ranged from book and magazine illustrations to murals at Tougaloo Southern Christian College, The American Museum of Natural History, the College of the City of New York, and the Golden State Mutual Life Insurance Company in Los Angeles.

Edmund Archer (1904–) was born in Richmond, Virginia, and attended the University of Virginia. He studied painting in New York at the Art Students League and later in Europe. His work is represented in the Whitney Museum and several other important American collections.

Romare Bearden (1914–) was born in Charlotte, North Carolina, and educated at New York University and the University of Pittsburgh. He studied painting at the American Arts School and the Art Students League. He began exhibiting at the Harlem Art Center in 1937, and since then his work has been shown in many leading galleries and museums.

Colleen Browning (1924–) entered art school in England at the age of fifteen. She has been a designer of stage and movie sets, and during World War II drew maps for the British War Office. She and her husband—the writer Geoffrey Wagner—came to America in the 1950's and lived in East Harlem, where she began her studies of Negro life. Her work has earned a place in many national exhibitions. She has won several prizes and has had many one-man shows. Recently she has been teaching art at the City College of New York.

Thomas Eakins (1844–1916) was a Philadelphian, who studied painting in France and Spain. In 1870 he became a teacher at the Pennsylvania Academy of Fine Arts. He painted his family and friends in their daily activities and later concentrated on portraits. The paintings of his Negro friends and neighbors, including his pupil Henry Ossawa Tanner, are among Eakins' most forceful character studies.

Albert Handell (1937–) had his first major New York showing at the age of twenty-nine. Born in Brooklyn, New York, he studied at the Art Students League from 1954 to 1958. He won his first award as a student and has earned several others since.

Robert Henri (1865–1928) was born in Cincinnati, and studied painting in Philadelphia and in Paris. In 1891, as a teacher at the Pennsylvania Academy of Fine Arts, he became the leader of a group of realist painters who depicted the streets and people of their city. With his group Henri moved in 1904 to New York, where they and other rebels against tradition became known as the "Ash Can School."

Winslow Homer (1836–1910) grew up in Cambridge, Massachusetts. At nineteen he was apprenticed to a lithographer. He began his career designing covers for popular songs and doing pictures of rural life for illustrated magazines. During the Civil War he went to army camps and to the front as an artist-correspondent for *Harper's Weekly*. In 1875 he painted Negro women and children in their homes at Petersburg, Virginia. Later, in the Caribbean, Homer did watercolors of Negroes. He spent the last seventeen years of his life on the Maine coast.

Nathaniel Jocelyn (1796–1881), born in New Haven, was one of the early abolitionists. In 1839 he painted the portrait of Joseph Cinqué, the African who led a successful revolt aboard the slave ship *Amistad*. When the Africans were stopped by an American ship and put on trial in New Haven for the murder of the *Amistad*'s captain, the abolitionists took up their defense, with Jocelyn aiding them. John Quincy Adams, the aged former President, won their freedom by his plea before the Supreme Court.

Eastman Johnson (1824–1906) was brought up in Maine and at sixteen was apprenticed to a Boston lithographer. In 1842 he returned to Maine and became a painter. He also worked in Boston and Washington, and later studied in Germany and the Netherlands. After 1858 he lived and worked in New York.

Hughie Lee-Smith (1915–   ) was born in Eustis, Florida, and studied at the Detroit Society of Arts and Crafts, the Cleveland Institute of Arts, and Wayne State University. His first recognition came in 1943 with a purchase award in Atlanta University's annual art competition. He became, after Henry O. Tanner, the second Negro artist to be elected to the National Academy of Design.

Alice Neel (19 –   ) was born in Pennsylvania, lived in Spanish Harlem for years, and now lives on the upper West Side of New York. She specializes in portraits of people of all kinds.

Ben Shahn (1898–1969) came to Brooklyn at the age of eight with his family, immigrants from Lithuania. At thirteen he was apprenticed to a lithographer. He studied at New York University, City College of New York, and the National Academy of Design, and traveled in Europe. His first major success came in 1932 with a series of paintings about the execution of Sacco and Vanzetti. During the 1930's Shahn worked as a photographer for the Farm Security Administration and painted murals for government buildings. Later he designed posters for the Office of War Information and for presidential election campaigns. He exhibited in many museums and galleries, and was a well known book illustrator. He lived in Roosevelt, New Jersey.

Symeon Shimin (1902–   ) came to this country from Russia with his family in 1912. At sixteen he worked for a commercial artist and attended art classes at night. His chief schooling came through visits to museums and galleries here and abroad. He has painted murals for the Department of Justice Building in Washington and the Post Office in Tonawanda, New York. During World War II he designed posters for government agencies. His work has been shown in galleries and museums, and his illustrations have appeared in many books and magazines.

John Wilson (1922–   ) is a Bostonian, and was a scholarship student at the Boston Museum of Fine Arts for five years. He also took a B.S. in Education at Tufts College. By the early 1940's he was gaining attention through prizes won in the first two National Negro Art Exhibits, and a Pepsi Cola award. The Paige traveling fellowship took him to Europe for two years of study. His paintings are in many collections, including those of Smith College, Atlanta University, and the Museum of Modern Art. He is a member of the faculty of The Boston Museum of Fine Arts.

Andrew Wyeth (1917–   ) was born in Chadds Ford, Pennsylvania, where he still lives. He was educated by his father, N. C. Wyeth, the noted magazine and book illustrator. His career as an artist began when he was very young, and for more than thirty years he has been painting the people and places near his home. Today he is one of America's most popular painters.

In describing how this book came to be, June Jordan wrote, "We do not see those we do not know. Love and all varieties of happy concern depend on the discovery of one's self in another. The question of every desiring heart is, thus, WHO LOOK AT ME? In a nation suffering fierce hatred, the question—race to race, man to man, and child to child—remains: WHO LOOK AT ME? *We answer with our lives.* Let the human eye begin unlimited embrace of human life."

A native of New York City, June Jordan was born in Harlem and grew up in the Bedford Stuyvesant section of Brooklyn. She studied at Barnard College and at the University of Chicago. Miss Jordan's poetry has appeared in several magazines and anthologies, and she is, herself, the editor of a collection of poetry by black Americans. Under the auspices of the Academy of American Poets, she has read her poetry at public schools in Minneapolis and New York City, and at the Guggenheim Museum in New York.

Miss Jordan has taught English at City College of the City University of New York, and at Connecticut College for Women. She also conducts a creative writing workshop for children. She has written numerous articles for *Esquire*, *Mademoiselle*, *The Nation*, and *The Urban Review*, ranging in topic from architecture and economics to education and equal protection under law.